T0020508

ASH AND PIKACHU:
POKÉMON HEROES

★ x1996 Kenny Abdo

Fly!
An Imprint of Abdo Zoom
abdobooks.com

abdobooks.com

Printed in the United States of America, North Mankato, Minnesota.
052020
092020

THIS BOOK CONTAINS RECYCLED MATERIALS

Photo Credits: Alamy, AP Images, Everette Collection, Flickr, iStock, Newscom, Shutterstock, ©Bryan Ochalla p.14 / CC BY-SA 2.0
Production Contributors: Kenny Abdo, Jennie Forsberg, Grace Hansen
Design Contributors: Dorothy Toth, Neil Klinepier

Library of Congress Control Number: 2019956182

Publisher's Cataloging-in-Publication Data

Names: Abdo, Kenny, author.
Title: Ash and Pikachu: Pokémon heroes / by Kenny Abdo
Other title: Pokémon heroes
Description: Minneapolis, Minnesota : Abdo Zoom, 2021 | Series: Video game heroes | Includes online resources and index.
Identifiers: ISBN 9781098221430 (lib. bdg.) | ISBN 9781644944172 (pbk.) | ISBN 9781098222413 (ebook) | ISBN 9781098222901 (Read-to-Me ebook)
Subjects: LCSH: Video game characters--Juvenile literature. | Pokémon (Game)-Juvenile literature. | Pikachu (Fictitious character)--Juvenile literature. | Nintendo video games--Juvenile literature. | Heroes--Juvenile literature.
Classification: DDC 794.8--dc23

TABLE OF CONTENTS

ASH & PIKACHU

Traveling the land and defeating foes, Ash and Pikachu are two of the most popular video game heroes in the world!

Pokémon is about the bond between a **trainer** and their little fighting monster. And there is no greater friendship than the one between Ash Ketchum and Pikachu.

PLAYER PROFILE

Satoshi Tajiri based Ash on himself. As a young boy, Tajiri liked exploring the outdoors. He also liked collecting and studying insects.

Pikachu's design was created by Atsuko Nishida and Ken Sugimori. Pikachu means Electricity-Crackling-Mice when translated into English. He is modeled after a mouse.

The word Pokémon comes from putting "pocket" and "monsters" together. In all, there are almost 900 **species** of Pokémon.

In *Pokémon* **lore**, Ash did not originally want Pikachu. He wanted Squirtle. But he overslept. Ash got the only Pokémon left, which was Pikachu!

Pikachu made his electrifying debut in the United States in 1996. He lit up the *Pokémon Red* and *Blue* games for Game Boy.

Ash has appeared in only one
Pokémon game, *Pokémon Puzzle
League*. It came out in 2000. Even so,
Guinness ranked Ash as the 37th best
all-time video game character.

Ash and Pikachu are stars of the big and small screens. They have appeared in 897 episodes of the *Pokémon* television series. They also starred together in 18 movies!

Pikachu has dominated all seven **generations** of *Pokémon* games, which span every type of gaming device imaginable. From Game Boys to arcade machines to playing cards, choosing Pikachu is a surefire win!

EXPANSION PACK

In all, there have been more than 120 *Pokémon* video games. *Pokémon Go* debuted in 2016 and was a worldwide hit. With **augmented reality** (AR) you can bring Pikachu with you anywhere!

The *Pokémon* TV show ran for 1,066 episodes. *Time* magazine called Pikachu "...the most recognized and beloved sidekicks in pop culture."

Pokémon is the highest **grossing** media **franchise** of all time. With $95 billion, it beats out Star Wars, Marvel, and Hello Kitty. *Pokémon*, the world chooses you!

GLOSSARY

augmented reality (AR) – an interactive experience combining the real-world enhanced by computer-generated visuals and sounds.

franchise – a series of related works each of which includes the same characters that interact in the same fictional universe.

generation – a stage of technological innovation and growth.

gross – to produce profit.

lore – a story handed down from person to person.

species – living things that are very much alike.

trainer – in *Pokémon*, a person who catches, trains, and battles with Pokémon.

ONLINE RESOURCES

Booklinks
NONFICTION NETWORK
FREE! ONLINE NONFICTION RESOURCES

To learn more about Ash and Pikachu, please visit **abdobooklinks.com** or scan this QR code. These links are routinely monitored and updated to provide the most current information available.

INDEX